I MISS MOM

Written by: Chiara Rucker

This book is dedicated
to my loving mother.
"Mom, I just want you
to know that I miss you
so much."
Keep Resting My Angel

Mom was my favorite person.

We did everything together.
We went shopping.

We baked cakes.

We played board games.

We even went to the fair together. We had so much fun.

Then one day, mom
was no longer there.

As the days passed, I became lonely and sad. I had no one to have fun with anymore.

My family would invite me to do things, but it still didn't feel the same without mom.

Some nights I could barely sleep!

Some days I felt happy.

Some days I felt sad.

I just wish I could be with my favorite person again! I miss mom!

To all who have experienced death...

Psalm 34:18

The Lord is close to the brokenhearted and saves those who are crushed in spirit.

Made in the USA
Middletown, DE
22 October 2022

13288647R00018